DON'T RETIRE...

Graduate!

THE WORKBOOK

ERIC D. BROTMAN, CFP ®

BROTMAN
Media Group
A division of Brotman Financial Group, Inc.

16 Greenmeadow Drive, Suite 201
Timonium, MD 21903

www.brotmanmedia.com

Eric@DontRetireGraduate.com

www.facebook.com/DontRetireGraduate/

ISBN: 978-1-7349701-4-2

Ordering Information:

Special discounts are available on quantity purchases by corporations, associations, and others. For details, contact Brotman Media at 410-252-4555.

INTRODUCTION

So many people want to reach financial independence and have no idea how to get there or what to do when they arrive. The financial world can be so complex and daunting that it's hard to know even where to start.

This workbook is designed to accompany the book Don't Retire…Graduate! and the online course by the same title, but it can also be used without those other resources. The content has been designed to be a blueprint for reaching financial independence through a series of assignments. In the book I refer to these assignments as "extra credit," but they are also foundational building blocks for financial success. The book and course are broken down into semesters to mirror a college curriculum with a double-major in financial independence and retirement readiness. The assignments won't be in a fully linear order in every reader's life, but they are meant to build on one another.

I hope you'll take the opportunity to start chipping away at the assignments that are relevant for you and to review the material in the book and course to help you along the way. A brief summary of the assignments begins on the next page.

SUMMARY OF EXTRA-CREDIT ASSIGNMENTS

FRESHMAN YEAR

Pg. 9 – Set a savings and investment target as a percentage of your income and make it happen. (Cash Management 101)

Pg. 13 – Take a full inventory of your debt balances and interest rates. (Debt Management 101)

Pg. 17 – If you have equity in your home, make sure you have a home equity line of credit (HELOC) in place for working capital, debt consolidation, and potential future opportunities. (Debt Management 102)

Pg.23 – Create a debt-reduction plan. (Debt Management 103)

Pg. 27 – Review all of your insurance coverages. (Risk Management & Protection 101)

Pg. 31 – Create a budget. (Cash Management 102)

Pg. 37 – Ask your financial advisor the list of important questions or use them to find the right financial advisor for you. (Financial Planning 101)

Pg. 45 – List your assets and liabilities to complete your initial inventory. (Financial Planning 102)

SOPHOMORE YEAR

Pg. 51 – Start building your savings nest egg if you're planning to buy a home. (Financial Planning 201)

JUNIOR YEAR

SENIOR YEAR

GRADUATION DAY

Freshman Year
Extra-Credit Assignments

Assignment 1

CASH MANAGEMENT 101

Choose a percentage of your annualized income as a savings and investment target and begin to pay yourself first with automatic deposits, contributions, or transfers to one or more accounts available to you. Challenge yourself to save at least 10 percent, and if you're ready for a stretch goal, shoot for 15 or 20 percent of your gross income as a starting point every month.

Note: Any funds being contributed by your employer as a match, a profit-sharing contribution, or any other form of deposit will count towards your percentage of savings. So if your employer matches 3 percent of your gross income into your 401(k)-assuming you make the 6 percent contribution by payroll deduction, that will count as 9 percent towards your overall savings target.

Before undertaking this extra-credit assignment, you'll want to make sure you are free of adverse debt and that you're aware of any matching or other employer contributions for which you are eligible, as this will impact the outcome of the assignment. If you have adverse debt, instead of setting a goal to save a percentage of your income, set a similar goal to pay excess principal to your debt as a percentage of your income. This will allow you to create wealth in the long term and will also help you reduce adverse interest payments and debt service in the short run.

Note: If you need assistance in creating a debt-reduction plan to complete this assignment in the most efficient and cost-effective way, complete Assignment 4 and then return to undertake Assignment 1.

To form a habit of paying yourself first, track your progress for the next 12 months on **Worksheet 1**.

WORKSHEET 1 — CASH MANAGEMENT 101

Monthly Savings Goal (%): _____

Month	Total Gross Income	Amount Saved/ Invested	% Saved/Invested	Check When Complete

Hopefully, this has started you on a good habit you can maintain for life. If you hit your target all 12 months, consider increasing your target for the next 12 months. If you're unable to hit your target for all 12 months, try to increase your income or reduce your spending and try again. Once you hit your savings target for 12 months in a row, it may be time to increase your target.

Assignment 2

DEBT MANAGEMENT 101

Take a full inventory of your debts (and if you are married, your spouse's debts). Make sure you know the full balances, the interest rates, the time to maturity, and any special considerations (like short-term, interest-free terms) for each debt.

You will use this extra-credit assignment to make major progress starting in the next course, and this one step will give you an excellent foundation for creating a strategy and plan for debt reduction.

Using **Worksheet 2**, make a list of all of your adverse debts, including credit cards and consumer debt, all 401(k) loans, any unfavorable or variable student loans, all margin loans, and most loans against life insurance policies.

Note: If you are making extra payments to a mortgage, a home equity line of credit, or any other collateralized loan, include that loan on Worksheet 2 as it may be helpful in designing your debt-reduction plan.

The description will be the name of the creditor or another way for you to identify the account.

The balance will be the amount due to pay the obligation in-full.

The typical payment is the amount you pay in a normal month. If your payment varies throughout the year, list the average payment.

The minimum payment is the amount on the statement which is required to be paid to avoid a penalty.

The interest rate is the monthly or annually calculated rate being charged on the account.

WORKSHEET 2 — DEBT MANAGEMENT 101

Description	Balance	Typical Monthly Payment	Minimum Payment Required	Interest Rate
	$	$	$	%
	$	$	$	%
	$	$	$	%
	$	$	$	%
	$	$	$	%
	$	$	$	%
	$	$	$	%
	$	$	$	%
	$	$	$	%
	$	$	$	%
	$	$	$	%
	$	$	$	%
	$	$	$	%
	$	$	$	%
	$	$	$	%
	$	$	$	%
	$	$	$	%
	$	$	$	%
	$	$	$	%

This worksheet will be used again to develop a debt-reduction plan in Assignment 4.

Assignment 3

DEBT MANAGEMENT 102

If you are a homeowner, consider getting an appraisal on your home to see how much equity is available, and explore options for a home equity line of credit (HELOC). Start with your present bank or credit union where you already maintain a relationship, but don't be afraid to shop for favorable terms. You don't need to have all of your borrowing with the same institution for any reason, so explore the options and get the best deal you can find.

If you have enough home equity to clean up any adverse consumer debt, consider this strategy as a step towards financial freedom. Note that even if you do not presently need to use the line for debt restructuring, having available credit is an excellent tool for emergencies and opportunities that arise in the future. It is always better to borrow money when you don't need it than when you do, because financial institutions can be hesitant to lend money to people favorably when they are in great need.

WORKSHEET 3 — DEBT MANAGEMENT 102

Home #1

Step 1:	Enter Fair Market Value (FMV):		$_____
Step 2:	Calculate 80% of FMV		$_____
	(FMV x 0.80)		$_____
Step 3:	List all debts/liabilities:		$_____
	1st Mortgage		$_____
	2nd Mortgage		$_____
	Home Equity Loan		$_____
	Home Equity LOC	+	$_____
	TOTAL:	=	$_____

Step 4:   Determine possible available resources.

If the answer in Step 2 is <u>greater than</u> the total in Step 3, calculate the difference between the two figures and enter it here: $_____

If the answer in Step 2 is <u>less than</u> the total in Step 3, there is unlikely to be available capital, so enter a $0 here: $_____

This figure will be an available resource if needed for debt consolidation, refinance, or restructuring in Assignment 4.

Repeat this exercise for a second home and any other real estate properties below and calculate the total available equity (up to 80 percent of fair market value) for all combined real estate holdings.

Home #2

Step 1:	Enter Fair Market Value (FMV):		$_____
Step 2:	Calculate 80% of FMV		$_____
	(FMV x 0.80)		$_____
Step 3:	List all debts/liabilities:		$_____
	1st Mortgage		$_____
	2nd Mortgage		$_____
	Home Equity Loan		$_____
	Home Equity LOC	+	$_____
	TOTAL:	=	$_____

Step 4:   Determine possible available resources.

If the answer in Step 2 is <u>greater than</u> the total in Step 3, calculate the difference between the two figures and enter it here: $\$$_____

If the answer in Step 2 is <u>less than</u> the total in Step 3, there is unlikely to be available capital, so enter a $0 here: $\$$_____

Other Real Estate Property:

Step 1:	Enter Fair Market Value (FMV):	$\$$_____
Step 2:	Calculate 80% of FMV	$\$$_____
	(FMV x 0.80)	$\$$_____
Step 3:	List all debts/liabilities:	$\$$_____
	1st Mortgage	$\$$_____
	2nd Mortgage	$\$$_____
	Home Equity Loan	$\$$_____
	Home Equity LOC	$+$ $\$$_____
	TOTAL:	$=$ $\$$_____

Step 4:   Determine possible available resources.

If the answer in Step 2 is <u>greater than</u> the total in Step 3, calculate the difference between the two figures and enter it here: $\$$_____

If the answer in Step 2 is <u>less than</u> the total in Step 3, there is unlikely to be available capital, so enter a $0 here: $\$$_____

Assignment 4

DEBT MANAGEMENT 103

If you completed your extra-credit assignment at the end of Debt Management 101 and you have your full inventory of debts, this assignment will be relatively easy. For this course's assignment, you now need to order your debts (as demonstrated in this chapter) and to determine a schedule for your debt reduction plan.

You can use a software program to assist you or you can accomplish this manually. Commit to a certain dollar figure to apply to debt every month that is greater than the sum of the minimum payments due. And apply all of that excess money each month to the principal on your outstanding debt with the highest after-tax interest rate.

You will begin to see your debt balance drop almost immediately. If you maintain discipline not only to stick to the schedule but also to avoid accumulating any new debts, you'll be on your way to freedom from debt.

Use *Worksheet 4* on the next page.

WORKSHEET 4 — DEBT MANAGEMENT 103

List all of your outstanding debts below ranked by the interest rate on each debt, starting with the highest interest rate debt first:

Description of Liability	Interest Rate	Total Balance	Minimum Payment	Actual Payment
	%	$	$	$
	%	$	$	$
	%	$	$	$
	%	$	$	$
	%	$	$	$
	%	$	$	$
	%	$	$	$
	%	$	$	$
	%	$	$	$
	%	$	$	$
	%	$	$	$
	%	$	$	$
	%	$	$	$
	%	$	$	$
	%	$	$	$
	%	$	$	$
	%	$	$	$

Assignment 5

RISK MANAGEMENT & PROTECTION 101

Having a complete financial plan means having a complete risk management plan as a key component, and no risk management plan can be complete without thorough insurance planning.

Your assignment is to review all of the insurance coverages discussed in this course and to consider utilizing a financial advisor to help you determine the adequacy and completeness of those coverages. If there are risks being covered that do not need to be covered, you can begin reducing or eliminating superfluous policies; while if there are risks you cannot bear that aren't covered, you'll want to start improving the moat around your financial castle with appropriate insurance solutions.

- ❏ **Automobile insurance**

- ❏ **Homeowners or renters insurance**

- ❏ **Liability insurance (personal and professional)**

- ❏ **Disability insurance**

- ❏ **Long-term care insurance (LTCI)**

- ❏ **Medical insurance**

- ❏ **Life insurance**

WORKSHEET 5 – RISK MANAGEMENT & PROTECTION 101

Insurance policy inventory:

Policy Type	Insurer	Policy #	Annual Premium	Reviewed with advisor/agent (Y/N?)

Assignment 6

CASH MANAGEMENT 102

The extra-credit assignment is to create a budget, if you don't have one, or to computerize your budget if it already exists and is manual. Track your income and expenses diligently for three months to get a sense of your current cash flows. Then use the data from your checkbook, credit card statements, bank statements, software program, or other system to get a sense of where you stand currently. You'll use that data to create (or update) your budget to ensure that you have maximized your cash flow. If possible, use this exercise to find a way to increase your long-term savings and investment plans by paying yourself first too!

WORKSHEET 6 – CASH MANAGEMENT 102

BUDGET WORKSHEET:

Fixed Expenses (monthly amount)	Month 1	Month 2	Month 3	Monthly Average
Home Mortgage/Rent	$	$	$	$
Other Mortgage	$	$	$	$
Real Estate Taxes	$	$	$	$
Maintenance Fees	$	$	$	$
Auto Insurance	$	$	$	$
Homeowner's Insurance	$	$	$	$
Life Insurance	$	$	$	$
Disability Insurance	$	$	$	$
Health Insurance	$	$	$	$
Other Insurance	$	$	$	$
Subscription Fees	$	$	$	$
Dues, Licenses, Fees, etc.	$	$	$	$
Bank Loans	$	$	$	$
Other Loans	$	$	$	$
Credit Cards	$	$	$	$
Support/Dependents	$	$	$	$
Other	$	$	$	$
Other	$	$	$	$
Other	$	$	$	$
Variable/Fixed Expenses	$	$	$	$
Food	$	$	$	$
Heat	$	$	$	$
Gas/Electricity	$	$	$	$
Telephone	$	$	$	$
Water, Sewer, & Garbage Collections	$	$	$	$
Laundry	$	$	$	$
House Help - Garden, Cleaning, Child Care	$	$	$	$
Basic Clothing	$	$	$	$
Medical, Doctors, Drugs	$	$	$	$
Car: Gas, Oil, Tolls, Parking	$	$	$	$
Repairs & Maintenance	$	$	$	$
Other	$	$	$	$
Other	$	$	$	$
Other				

Discretionary Expenses	$	$	$	$
Entertainment	$	$	$	$
Vacations	$	$	$	$
Education	$	$	$	$
Discretionary Clothing	$	$	$	$
Contributions	$	$	$	$
Recreation	$	$	$	$
Health Care, Beauty Care	$	$	$	$
Incidentals	$	$	$	$
Other	$	$	$	$
Other	$	$	$	$
Other	$	$	$	$

Assignment 7

FINANCIAL PLANNING 101

The extra-credit assignment for this course is dependent on whether or not you already have a professional engagement with a financial advisor.

If you have a financial advisor currently, ask him or her the questions addressed in this course. If you are unsatisfied or uncomfortable with any of those answers, consider getting a second opinion.

If you do not yet have a financial advisor, ask your friends, family members, colleagues, or other legal or tax advisors for one or more names of their trusted advisors and begin the process of interviewing a few to find the right fit for you.

Completing this extra-credit assignment may not ensure that you find the right advisor for you, but it will certainly assist in beginning the process of engaging a professional appropriate for your financial and personal situation.

WORKSHEET 7 — FINANCIAL PLANNING 101

Interview your current financial advisor (or one or more potential financial advisors) to learn more about the items discussed in the book. You can make copies of this sheet, if needed, or just list your answers below:

1. What services does the advisor provide personally?

2. How often will the advisor meet with you?

3. How much communication can you expect on an ongoing basis?

4. Does your advisor have other team members who are available to you?

5. Who are the typical clients of this advisor or firm?

6. What is the advisor's planning and investment philosophy?

7. Does the advisor represent specific companies or products?

8. How does the advisor select specialists?

9. Will you have online access to your planning and accounts?

10. Does the firm expect to grow, and how might that impact your relationship moving forward?

11. What is the cost of doing business with this firm?

12. Does the firm utilize a commercial custodian or other entity to safeguard client assets?

Assignment 8

FINANCIAL PLANNING 102

The extra-credit assignment for this course is to begin your financial inventory process by simply listing all of your assets on one column or sheet of paper and all of your liabilities on another column or sheet of paper.

Once you know your net worth, you will have the "You are here" sticker for your own financial journey map. This will allow you to begin taking the next steps towards reaching financial independence, including an examination of your cash flow and improvements to your personal budget, balance sheet, and income statement.

WORKSHEET 8 — FINANCIAL PLANNING 102

Step 1: List a description and dollar value of each asset and liability below and add them up to put a total at the bottom of the worksheet.

Assets		Liabilities	
Description	$ Amount	Description	$ Amount
	$		$
	$		$
	$		$
	$		$
	$		$
	$		$
	$		$
	$		$
	$		$
	$		$
	$		$
	$		$
	$		$
	$		$
	$		$
	$		$
	$		$
	$		$

Step 2: Subtract total liabilities from total assets to calculate your net worth.

Enter your net worth here: $_____

Sophomore Year
Extra-Credit Assignments

Assignment 9

FINANCIAL PLANNING 201

If you are contemplating a first home, or even a move to a new home, your extra-credit assignment is to begin saving for the down payment and other initial costs to make the big move. Open a simple savings account or money market and start adding to the balance every month in an amount that is likely to be your increased cost after a potential move.

Completion of this assignment will serve two purposes. First, it will begin building your nest egg to allow for the down payment, closing costs, and moving expenses to be made from cash and not borrowed (hopefully, also eliminating the need to pay PMI). And second, by saving the additional amount each month in this way, you'll be able to practice your budgeting by living with the anticipated higher expenses so that you'll have a sense of how affordable life will be after you identify a new home and make the move.

WORKSHEET 9 — FINANCIAL PLANNING 201

Use these worksheets to estimate the total cost to purchase a house assuming various down payment percentages. Compare multiple houses based on purchase price and down payment amounts.

Purchase Price of Potential Houses	Down Payment (assume 20% of purchase price)	Closing Costs (assume 3% of purchase price)	Total estimated amount due at settlement (Down Payment + Closing Costs)
$	$	$	$
$	$	$	$
$	$	$	$
$	$	$	$
$	$	$	$

Purchase Price of Potential Houses	Down Payment (assume 10% of purchase price)	Closing Costs (assume 3% of purchase price)	Total estimated amount due at settlement (Down Payment + Closing Costs)
$	$	$	$
$	$	$	$
$	$	$	$
$	$	$	$
$	$	$	$

Purchase Price of Potential Houses	Down Payment (assume 3% of purchase price)	Closing Costs (assume 3% of purchase price)	Total estimated amount due at settlement (Down Payment + Closing Costs)
$	$	$	$
$	$	$	$
$	$	$	$
$	$	$	$
$	$	$	$

If you have the available cash for the total estimated amount due, you can afford to make the initial purchase. *Note that the estimated amount required to make an initial purchase is only one consideration for a home purchase, and you'll also need to consider the affordability of initial expenses like improvements, furnishings and ongoing expenses including mortgage payments, real estate taxes, insurance, maintenance and upkeep.*

If you do not have the available cash for the total estimated amount due, you cannot yet afford to make the initial purchase and will need to save for the initial amount due. To calculate your savings plan for this amount, take the following steps:

Step 1: Take the total estimated amount due: $_____

Step 2: List your available cash resources: $_____

Step 3: Line 2 from Line 1 to determine your shortfall: $_____

Step 4: List the amount you're able to save towards your home purchase each month:

$_____

Step 5: Divide Line 4 into Line 3 to determine the number of months it will take to save the estimated amount. Assume no interest on these funds: _____

Step 6: Use your existing savings account or open a new one and save the amount listed in Step 4 each month for the number of months determined in Step 5.

Step 7: Once you have reached your target estimated amount…go house hunting!

Assignment 10

FINANCIAL PLANNING 202

This course's extra-credit assignment will vary based upon your marital status.

If you are already married and have not already done so, consider hiring a financial advisor to walk you and your spouse through a combined financial planning process. This will open communication and allow for coordination of plans and the establishment of shared goals for the future.

If you are planning to become or are already engaged, your assignment is to hold an open and honest discussion with your partner about your finances and possibly to engage a financial advisor together to assist.

If you are single and have no immediate plans to consider marriage, your assignment is simply to take care of your own financial affairs in such a way that when and if you meet the right person, you'll be very comfortable sharing with him or her with full transparency.

Use the next page to debrief after your conversation.

WORKSHEET 10 – FINANCIAL PLANNING 202

Make notes about your observations and feelings here–especially any *a-ha!* moments or big takeaways–and then create an action plan and a follow-up schedule to make sure these conversations are worthwhile and can make an impact on you both. You may want to work on this together, or each of you may want to make your own notes to then discuss together.

<u>*A-HA!* MOMENTS</u>

<u>BIG TAKEAWAYS</u>

<u>ACTION STEPS</u>

FOLLOW-UP SCHEDULE

FOLLOW-UP SCHEDULE

Assignment 11
FINANCIAL PLANNING 203

Whether you already have children or you're considering having children, spend time with your spouse talking about some of the financial matters described in this course. Make sure you are on the same page in terms of your own employment, childcare, public vs. private education, and college funding goals.

Becoming a parent is one of the most rewarding decisions people can make but also is one of the most challenging and expensive. Open communication in advance can help manage everyone's expectations and avoid some of the surprises that occur when you are suddenly a mom or dad.

Topics to discuss may include:

- Education Expenses
- Public vs. Private Education
- Employment
- College Funding Goals
- Childcare

Use the next page to debrief after your conversation.

WORKSHEET 11 – FINANCIAL PLANNING 203

Make notes about your observations and feelings here–especially any *a-ha!* moments or big takeaways–and then create an action plan and a follow-up schedule to make sure these conversations are worthwhile and can make an impact on you both. You may want to work on this together, or each of you may want to make your own notes to then discuss together.

A-HA! MOMENTS

BIG TAKEAWAYS

ACTION STEPS

FOLLOW-UP SCHEDULE

Assignment 12

FINANCIAL INDEPENDENCE 201

This course contains so much dense material that choosing a single extra-credit assignment isn't easy. Instead of a single assignment, this course has three different options and I encourage you to choose one.

If you were to take only one action as a result of completing this course, it would be to consider one of these three next steps:

- If you have never used a financial advisor, consider meeting with one and asking for some feedback on your existing portfolio allocation. You can still be a DIY investor but getting another set of eyes on your statements once in a while might prove to be invaluable.

- If you currently use an advisor, particularly one who espouses market timing, stock picking, or potentially expensive active management, consider getting a second opinion. Much like the DIY investor, you don't have to change advisors but you might benefit from another perspective on your portfolio, just as you might benefit from a second opinion if facing a medical decision.

- Consider reading one or more of the recommended books on behavioral risks and investing listed earlier in the course (refer to the text). You may find them enlightening and might even identify some of your own behaviors that, if corrected or adjusted, could benefit your investment plan.

WORKSHEET 12 – FINANCIAL INDEPENDENCE 201

Make notes about your conversation(s) with your existing and/or potential financial advisor(s)–especially about your overall portfolio strategy and suitability and any material weaknesses in your present investment portfolio–and then create an action plan and a follow-up schedule to make sure you take appropriate actions within a reasonable amount of time.

OVERALL PORTFOLIO STRATEGY & SUITABILITY

MATERIAL WEAKNESSES IN YOUR PORTFOLIO

ACTION STEPS

FOLLOW-UP SCHEDULE

FOLLOW-UP SCHEDULE

Assignment 13

FINANCIAL INDEPENDENCE 202

Your final extra-credit assignment for your sophomore year is to analyze your existing portfolio holdings. Of the asset classes described in this course, determine which ones you own presently and what percentage of your portfolio is in each asset class. Once you have taken this portfolio inventory, consider meeting with a financial advisor to determine if your current allocation is appropriate for you or if you could benefit from adding or eliminating asset classes or holding a different allocation.

1. Cash and Cash Equivalents

2. Fixed Income Securities

3. Equities

4. Alternative Investments

WORKSHEET 13 – FINANCIAL INDEPENDENCE 202

Step 1: List all current holdings by asset class, including the institution where the asset is held, the name, description, or ticker symbol for the asset, and the market value for each asset. Total the market value column for each asset class below.

Cash & Cash Equivalents:

Institution where Held	Asset Name/Ticker	Market Value
		$
		$
		$
		$
		$
		$
		$
		$
TOTAL VALUE:		$

Fixed Income Securities:

Institution where Held	Asset Name/Ticker	Market Value
		$
		$
		$
		$
		$
		$
		$
		$
TOTAL VALUE:		$

Equities:

Institution where Held	Asset Name/Ticker	Market Value
		$
		$
		$
		$
		$
		$
		$
		$
TOTAL VALUE:		$

Alternative Investments:

Institution where Held	Asset Name/Ticker	Market Value
		$
		$
		$
		$
		$
		$
		$
		$
TOTAL VALUE:		$

Step 2: Add together the total value of each of the four asset classes to come up with the market value of the working assets in your portfolio.

Step 3: Divide each of the individual asset class' total value by the sum of the values from Step 2 to come up with a percentage of each asset class in your portfolio:

Asset Class	Percentage of Overall Portfolio
Cash & Cash Equivalents	%
Fixed Income Securities	%
Equities	%
Alternatives	%
TOTAL ALLOCATION:	**100%**

With the help of your financial advisor, determine if your overall allocation is appropriate for you and your present goals and objectives, and make changes if needed.

Junior Year
Extra-Credit Assignments

Assignment 14

FINANCIAL INDEPENDENCE 101

If you are enrolled in your employer's qualified retirement plan, or you are eligible for but not yet enrolled in the plan, request a copy of the Summary Plan Description (SPD) and read it. If you have questions, ask your HR department or plan administrator to answer them or review the SPD with your financial advisor.

You may not be taking full advantage of your employer's plan provisions and may be leaving a potential tax-deferred raise on the table by doing so. Once you know the plan's rules, you can arrange to utilize the plan in an optimal way that helps you reach financial independence.

WORKSHEET 14 – FINANCIAL INDEPENDENCE 301

Answer the following questions below related to your qualified retirement plan to determine any action steps required and a timeline to reach them.

Summary Plan Descriptions for current and prior employer plans:

Employer Name	SPD Requested? (Yes / No)	SPD Received? (Yes / No)	SPD Reviewed? (Yes / No)

Active Plan #1

Current employee contribution % of salary: _____%

Current employer contribution % of salary: _____%

Goal for employee contribution % of salary: _____%

If you have not maximized your contributions or at least achieved your own goal to save a certain percentage of your salary, what is the plan to get there? Can you increase your percentage every year by some amount until you hit your target?

Current %: _____%

Starting next January: _____%

Starting in 2 years: _____%

Starting in 3 years: _____%

Starting in 4 years: _____%

Starting in 5 years: _____%

Active Plan #2

Current employee contribution % of salary: _____%

Current employer contribution % of salary: _____%

Goal for employee contribution % of salary: _____%

If you have not maximized your contributions or at least achieved your own goal to save a certain percentage of your salary, what is the plan to get there? Can you increase your percentage every year by some amount until you hit your target?

Current %: _____%

Starting next January: _____%

Starting in 2 years: _____%

Starting in 3 years: _____%

Starting in 4 years: _____%

Starting in 5 years: _____%

Assignment 15

RISK MANAGEMENT & PROTECTION 202

The extra-credit assignment for this course is to have a family discussion about long-term care plans for all adults over age 45.

If you are uncomfortable leading a family discussion like this one, ask your financial advisor to help you. If it is geographically possible, try to have everyone together in the same room. These are hard conversations and the phone isn't the best means to handle them, especially if some of your relatives are already advanced in age.

The cost of care is so extreme that it can impact several generations of a family and the stress on family caregivers is intense, especially when a family member has Alzheimer's disease or another form of cognitive impairment. The right strategy can make a big difference to everyone in the family.

WORKSHEET 15 – RISK MANAGEMENT & PROTECTION 202

Make notes about your observations and feelings here–especially any *a-ha!* moments or big takeaways–and then create an action plan and a follow-up schedule to make sure these conversations are worthwhile and can make an impact on you and your extended family. Ideally, work on this together as a group to try to get everyone on the same page as much as possible.

A-HA! MOMENTS

BIG TAKEAWAYS

ACTION STEPS

FOLLOW-UP SCHEDULE

Assignment 16

RISK MANAGEMENT & PROTECTION 203

For this course, the extra-credit assignment will depend if you currently have executed estate planning documents or not.

If you do not yet have these documents, the assignment is to meet with an attorney in your home state to draft and execute the documents described in the course that are appropriate for you. Skip directly to *Worksheet 16*.

If you already have executed estate planning documents, before moving to *Worksheet 16*, review them in light of the material in this course and consider meeting with your existing attorney or an alternate one in your home state if any of the following scenarios applies to you. Check the circle on the left of each statement which applies to you:

○ Your documents are more than five years old.

○ You have changed your state of residence since the execution of your current documents.

○ One or more of your named responsible parties has died or has become less optimal due to geography, illness, or any other reason.

○ You have gotten married or divorced or had children born since the execution of your current documents.

○ One or more of your grown children has gotten married or divorced or had children born since the execution of your current documents.

○ Any other material life changes have occurred, including dramatic change in your personal wealth or health or a change in your personal wishes or family dynamics.

If one or more of the circles above is checked, move on to *Worksheet 16*. If none of the circles above is checked, you may be able to skip *Worksheet 16*.

WORKSHEET 16 – RISK MANAGEMENT & PROTECTION 203

Use this worksheet to make sure that the process of updating your estate plan moves forward.

Have you scheduled a meeting with one or more attorneys to determine who you may want to engage? If no, begin the process of finding appropriate attorneys in your home state before continuing. Contact one or more and get the meeting(s) scheduled ASAP.

Complete this chart for each member of your household:

Adult #1

Document	Meeting held to allow drafting? (Y/N)	Draft received & reviewed? (Y/N)	Document executed? (Y/N)
Will			
Durable Financial Power of Attorney			
Advanced Medical Directive			
Living Will			
Trust/Other			
Trust/Other			

Adult #2:

Document	Meeting held to allow drafting? (Y/N)	Draft received & reviewed? (Y/N)	Document executed? (Y/N)
Will			
Durable Financial Power of Attorney			
Advanced Medical Directive			
Living Will			
Trust/Other			
Trust/Other			

Children:

Name	Age 18+? (Y/N)	Financial POA executed (if over age 18)? (Y/N)	Medical Directive executed (if over age 18)? (Y/N)

Once these have all been executed, verify your beneficiary designations and asset titling as described in the book and make sure to update these again as needed.

Assignment 17

RISK MANAGEMENT & PROTECTION 203

Your assignment for this course is to take a complete inventory of your beneficiary designations for all of your family's accounts. Note that you'll want to know not only the primary beneficiaries but also the contingent beneficiaries (in the event your primary beneficiaries predecease you).

The types of accounts that often have beneficiaries you'll want to verify include:

○ Qualified retirement plans

○ IRA accounts, including Roth IRAs, SEP IRAs, and SIMPLE IRAs

○ Life insurance policies

○ Transfer on Death (TOD) accounts

○ Employee benefits—not only life insurance but also deferred compensation or profit-sharing plans

Once you have completed the extra credit from this course and the last course, you'll be able to verify that both your will and your beneficiaries are set up properly to avoid all types of challenging problems when you die.

WORKSHEET 17 — RISK MANAGEMENT & PROTECTION 203

Account type	Owner(s) on title	Primary beneficiaries named	Contingent beneficiaries named

Senior Year
Extra-Credit Assignments

Assignment 18

FINANCIAL INDEPENDENCE 401

This course's extra-credit assignment should be fun. Regardless of your present age, write down up to a dozen things that you'd like to make sure to do during your lifetime.

These can be places to visit (think Bora Bora), adventures to try (skydiving, anyone?), or friendships or other relationships you want to cultivate or restore. If you reduce these things to writing, you are far more likely to make them happen.

Remember also that this list is not made in stone. It can change as your life changes. It might even be something worth revisiting and updating every year or two to make sure it remains relevant and that you're starting to check off the items you've completed to make room for new ones.

WORKSHEET 18 — FINANCIAL INDEPENDENCE 401

Personal "Bucket List" Items:

Priority	Action/Activity/ Goal	Scheduled? Y/N	Completed? Y/N
1			
2			
3			
4			
5			
6			
7			
8			
9			
10			
11			
12			

Assignment 19

RETIREMENT READINESS 401

For this course's extra-credit assignment, go back to the balance sheet and income statement that you created several semesters ago and determine the withdrawal rate you would need if you wanted to retire *immediately*.

As a reminder, the calculation looks like this:

1. Take your total gross income, including any employer-paid contributions or matches.

2. Subtract the amount you are saving or investing annually (again, including the employer-paid amount).

3. Subtract the amount of any costs that could be eliminated immediately. This could be your kids' tuitions (if they are about to graduate), your mortgage payment (if you plan to pay it off, downsize, or use a reverse mortgage), or any other costs that you could eliminate today if you retired immediately.

4. Take the remaining figure (gross income minus savings minus excess expenses) and divide it by your total available working assets. This will yield a percentage.

5. Note whether the percentage would allow you to retire today under the total return method, the asset segregation method, the annuitization method, or not at all.

If you aren't ready to retire or this percentage isn't optimal for you, use it as a measuring rod and challenge yourself to reduce this percentage every year during your remaining accumulation years until you're ready to claim financial independence and graduate.

WORKSHEET 19 – RETIREMENT READINESS 401

Answer the following questions in preparation for the <u>quantifiable</u> aspects of retirement readiness:

What would your required withdrawal rate be if you retired entirely today?

Based on your present standard of living and expenses, and adjusting for inflation, what is the target (or ideal) amount of money you would need to be financially independent and ready to retire *financially* today?

If you are already at that figure, congratulations! If not, how long will it take to hit your target based on reasonable inflation and return assumptions?

What are the next steps to take to reach that target in the time indicated in the last question (or less!)?

.

Assignment 20

RETIREMENT READINESS 402

Your extra-credit assignment is to take a hard look at your present residence. Consider access to bedrooms, bathrooms, laundry rooms, and other common spaces. While your home might be close to your present employment, consider your proximity to family, friends, hobbies, and hospitals, and determine if the geography is likely to be ideal once you aren't commuting to your present job.

If you are 65 years old, ask yourself candidly if an 85-year-old version of you could realistically manage in your present home and use **Worksheet 20A** to document the challenges or issues which may need to be addressed.

If you can age in-place and have proximity to people and places likely to be important during your retirement years, check the box and make sure your financial plan takes staying put into consideration.

If you can't age in-place or expect you'll need or want to move for some other reason when you graduate into your retirement, discuss this reality with your spouse, extended family, and financial advisor, and make sure your plan incorporates the costs of a relocation. Relocation costs include the expenses to prepare a home to be sold, to sell it, to buy a new home, to furnish and modify it and to make the physical move.

Note: For younger people who aren't five years or fewer to your planned retirement, you can skip this assignment, unless you have parents or grandparents who are living, in which case your assignment is much tougher than it is for the older folks completing this course.

Your assignment is to open a dialogue with your parents, grandparents, or other more senior relatives and to familiarize them with the concepts in this course. A little insight for them might make a tremendous difference—for them and for you. Use **Worksheet 20B** for this conversation.

WORKSHEET 20A — RETIREMENT READINESS 402

Room/Area of your present home	Issues or challenges to address or resolve (if resolvable)
Geographic concerns	How does your present home allow for proximity and access?
Family	
Friends	
Hobbies/Interests	
Medical Care/ Hospitals	
Other Priorities	

Based on the list of issues and concerns about your present home and the benefits and challenges of your present geography, can you reasonably age in-place in your present home or will you need to plan for a move at some point during your lifetime?

If you need to consider a move, list the action items and priorities to consider and start to create a timeline to address them.

WORKSHEET 20B – RETIREMENT READINESS 402

Make notes about your observations and feelings here–especially any *a-ha!* moments or big takeaways–and then create an action plan and a follow-up schedule to make sure these conversations are worthwhile and can make an impact on you and your extended family. Ideally, work on this together as a group to try to get everyone on the same page as much as possible.

A-HA! MOMENTS

BIG TAKEAWAYS

ACTION STEPS

FOLLOW-UP SCHEDULE

Assignment 21

RETIREMENT READINESS 403

The extra-credit assignment for this course may be more suited for a yoga or meditation practice than for a retirement readiness course.

Breathe.

You have major decisions to make, and some are time sensitive, so pace yourself and plan ahead. Making any of these decisions under duress will be especially hard and some of that anxiety can be relieved by proper planning.

So breathe. Give yourself the space and time to think about these decisions in advance. You've earned it.

Graduation Day
Extra-Credit Assignments

Assignment 22

GRADUATION DAY

Your final extra-credit assignment may be the most challenging but also the most rewarding of all the work you've done since enrolling at Retire U.

Think about the messages in this chapter and how you can make a difference and leave a legacy that is far more impactful than money. Answer the following big questions and prepare to act on every one of them—and to start soon.

1. **What do you want to be when you grow up?**

2. **What legacy do you want to leave?**

3. **How do you want to be remembered?**

4. **How can you leave behind your values and not just your items of value?**

Based on your answers to the questions above, list the action items and priorities to consider and start to create a timeline to address them.

POST GRADUATION

Please remember to share how this book helped you formulate your own plans to graduate into retirement. Send me an e-mail at Eric@DontRetireGraduate.com and tell your story about how you used this book to work your way to graduation day and financial independence. I'd love to hear your success stories!

Please also consider writing a review on Amazon or other book sites to help spread the word about your new vision for retirement–as a graduation and not a retreat.

Toss your cap in the air! You did it!

www.ingramcontent.com/pod-product-compliance
Lightning Source LLC
Chambersburg PA
CBHW051756200326
41597CB00025B/4575